David Robinson

SPORTS REPORTS

David Robinson
Star Center

Glen Macnow

Z0040090   5/95

ENSLOW PUBLISHERS, INC.

Bloy St. & Ramsey Ave.	P.O. Box 38
Box 777	Aldershot
Hillside, N.J. 07205	Hants GU12 6BP
U.S.A.	U.K.

Dedicated to Dorothy Goodstein,
who still has more boundless energy
than an entire NBA team.

Library of Congress Cataloging-in-Publication Data

Macnow, Glen.
      David Robinson : star center / Glen Macnow.
         p. cm. – (Sports reports)
      Includes bibliographical references (p.) and index.
      ISBN 0-89490-483-3
      1. Robinson, David, 1965– —Juvenile literature. 2. Basketball players—
United States—Biography—Juvenile literature. [1. Robinson, David, 1965– .
2. Basketball players. 3. Afro-Americans–Biography.] I. Title. II. Series.
GV884.R615M33 1994
796.323'092–dc20
[B]   94-15647
                                                                                           CIP
                                                                                            AC

Printed in the United States of America

10 9 8 7 6 5 4 3 2 1

Photo Credits: Nathaniel Butler, NBA, pp. 11, 72; Barry Gossage, NBA, pp.
8, 15, 19, 26, 29, 35, 40, 42, 50, 53, 57, 61, 65, 67, 82, 88; Jon Soohoo, NBA, pp.
24, 36, 46, 74, 76, 91; Paul White, NBA, p. 93.

Cover Illustration: Art Foxall, NBA Photos.

Contents

Chapter 1

A Dream Come True

More than 14,000 contestants took part in the 1992 Summer Olympics in Barcelona, Spain. They came from 172 different countries. Truly, these were the world's greatest athletes—men and women, runners and swimmers, boxers and baseball players.

But twelve of the Olympians stole most of the headlines. They were the members of the United States men's basketball team. The squad was dubbed the "Dream Team," and it was a good nickname. These dozen players combined so much talent that it seemed such a group could only exist in someone's dreams.

There was Michael Jordan, the acrobatic superstar from the Chicago Bulls. And Larry Bird, who was perhaps the best clutch shooter in the sport's history. And Charles Barkley, the thundering dunker

Although Robinson usually competes against Patrick Ewing, the two NBA stars shared duties as center for the 1992 U.S. Olympic "Dream Team."

who could steal rebounds from men eight inches taller than him.

At center, there were two all-stars from the National Basketball Association (NBA): Patrick Ewing of the New York Knicks and David Robinson of the San Antonio Spurs. Ewing and Robinson, both seven-footers, split time in the Olympic games.

"How can we lose with those two guys in the middle?" wondered teammate Magic Johnson, the great play-making guard from the Los Angeles Lakers. "Patrick's power will keep the other team from scoring inside. David can do so many things so well means that no one will be able to stop him."[1]

Johnson compared the team to the world's best musical band, in which Madonna, Michael Jackson, Bruce Springsteen, and Frank Sinatra are all singing. Who wouldn't want to see that?

In fact, everyone was eager to see just how dominant the Dream Team could be. In the pre-Olympic tournament held in July 1992, America's best won their five games by an average of 51 points. In one crushing victory over Brazil, Robinson scored 21 points, grabbed 13 rebounds, and blocked 5 shots. Afterward, Brazilian center Michael Souza—who spent the game trying to battle Robinson—called David the best center in the world. He had even nicer things to say about the Dream Team, calling them "the team of the universe. Maybe in another galaxy, if they play basketball in other galaxies, there is a team to beat them. But not here."[2]

To many, it seemed that America was sending twelve pounds of glitter to capture one ounce of Olympic gold. After all, professional basketball players had never competed in the Olympics before. That job was always left to the country's best college players. But these Dream Teamers considered themselves to be on a mission. Basketball was invented in the United States. It was perfected there. They wanted to prove that the best basketball is still played there.

No player had more to prove than David Robinson. Of the dozen Dream Team members, only Robinson had been a member of America's 1988 basketball squad. That team went to the Olympics in Seoul, South Korea, as a heavy favorite to win the gold medal. But, in a shocking semifinal game, it lost, 82–76, to the Soviet Union. It marked just the second time in Olympic history that the United States' basketball team had failed to come in first.

For Robinson, the 1988 loss was the lowest moment of his life. At that point, he was an officer in the U.S. Navy. He had finished a brilliant college career but had not yet started playing as a professional with the San Antonio Spurs. As America's top player, he was seen as the leader of the 1988 team. When it lost, David Robinson took much of the heat.

So he viewed the 1992 Olympics as a rescue mission. It was a chance to rescue the gold medal, and also a chance to rescue his own reputation a little bit.

Losing in 1988, Robinson said, "was more of a shock than anything. It was so hard to believe. But this second chance is the greatest. You don't usually get another opportunity, and with this team, you've got to feel good going in. But we all realize that it would be a very long and bad summer if we came home with anything less than the gold medal."[3]

Not to worry. The Dream Team went to Barcelona and continued to dominate its opponents as if they were grade-school clubs. The question was never whether these twelve superstars would win but rather how much they would run up the score. In fact, the club was so talented that other teams didn't even feel disappointed about losing. Instead, many said they felt honored just to have the chance to play against the world's best. Sometimes, players from losing teams would ask the Americans for their autographs and a chance to pose together in pictures. After one game, the center from the squad representing Angola asked if he could have Robinson's Olympic jersey as a souvenir. David cheerfully agreed. On August 8, 1992, the Dream

Robinson moves in to shoot. In his second appearance in the Olympics in 1992, he tried hard to bring the gold home for America.

Team—the greatest collection of basketball talent on earth—played Croatia for the gold medal. Prince Carlos of Spain sat in the front row, cheering every move made by the Americans. Other famous faces were in the crowd: actors Arnold Schwarzenegger and Jack Nicholson, movie director Spike Lee, basketball legend Julius Erving.

What they saw was a romp. The Americans spotted Croatia an early lead, 25–23, and then got serious. The Dream Teamers scored six straight baskets, and Robinson came in off the bench to tighten up the defense. Quickly, the U.S. squad began to run away with the game. In the end, the score was 117–85.

Michael Jordan led with 22 points. Charles Barkley had 17. Robinson, playing about half the game, had 9 points. He made all three of his field goal attempts and played terrific under the boards. On one memorable play early in the second half, David leaped to block a shot by Croatian forward Franjo Arapovic. While still in the air, he batted the loose ball to a running Barkley. Seconds later, Barkley finished the play with a rim-rattling dunk.

Afterward, America's Olympians crowded onto a podium while gold medals were hung around their necks. They celebrated like kids on Christmas morning. Charles Barkley and Magic Johnson

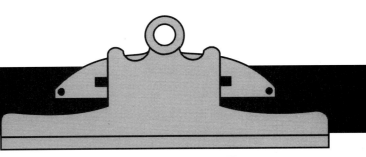

STATS

David was a proud member of the 1992 United States men's Olympic basketball team. The other players on that "Dream Team" were:

Name	Position	Height	NBA club
Charles Barkley	Forward	6'5"	Phoenix Suns
Larry Bird	Forward	6'9"	Boston Celtics
Clyde Drexler	Guard	6'7"	Portland Trail Blazers
Patrick Ewing	Center	7'0"	New York Knicks
Magic Johnson	Guard	6'10"	Los Angeles Lakers
Michael Jordan	Guard	6'6"	Chicago Bulls
Chris Laettner	Forward	6'11"	Minnesota Timberwolves
Karl Malone	Forward	6'9"	Utah Jazz
Chris Mullin	Forward	6'7"	Golden State Warriors
Scott Pippen	Forward	6'7"	Chicago Bulls
John Stockton	Guard	6'1"	Utah Jazz

hugged. Larry Bird danced a little jig. Robinson, the tallest member of the team, stood in the back, smiling. He was quieter than his teammates, but, maybe, he was the happiest of all. He alone had played on a losing Olympic team. Now, with a second chance, he had brought home the first-place medal. He—and his teammates—had proven themselves to be the best in the world.

Throughout his life, Robinson has proven himself the best at most everything he has tried. As a child, he was an excellent student and a fine musician. Sports was something he viewed as fun but didn't take seriously. In fact, David did not play organized basketball until his final year of high school. But in that one year, he played well enough to draw the interest of coaches from some of the best college programs in the country.

David chose to go to college at the U.S. Naval Academy in Annapolis, Maryland. He was attracted by the academics, not the basketball. He wanted to study electronics, something he had shown an interest in since he built a television by himself at the age of sixteen. His B-plus average at the academy shows what a good student he was.

But basketball worked out to be something special. David grew six inches—from six feet seven inches to seven feet one inch—during his years in the Navy. He was always a graceful athlete, especially good at gymnastics. The sudden growth spurt turned him into the top college player in the country. By the time he finished his college career in 1987, David owned thirty-three Naval Academy records and three all-time records for any player at any college. He was named the best college player in the country in 1986–87. Along the way, he earned the nickname, "The Admiral," a tribute to his standing in the Navy and his standing among other players.

At seven feet one inch, David Robinson has the height and grace to be one of the NBA's top centers.

Since finishing his military commitment, "The Admiral" has sailed on to the NBA. He joined the San Antonio Spurs in 1989 and was voted the league's top rookie that season. He made the all-star team in each of his first four seasons. And he helped build the Spurs from one of the worst teams in the NBA to one of the best.

What Robinson brings to the game is versatility, which means he can do many things very well. He is the only player in the NBA who year after year ranks among the top ten in five categories: scoring, rebounding, steals, blocked shots, and field goal percentage. He is perhaps the only seven-footer in history who can slam dunk the ball on one play, drib-ble-drive on the next, and pull up for a twenty-foot jump shot on the next. This David, truly, is a Goliath.

When an opponent faces the Admiral, said

Houston Rockets center Hakeem Olajuwon, "You are playing your toughest competition. You have to play offense, you have to play defense, and you have to work with both hands and both feet. It's very physical. You have to be at your peak."[4]

After just a few seasons in the pros, Robinson is considered to be the best defensive center since the great Bill Russell retired in 1969. With many seasons left to play, he may someday be considered the best ever.

He is also one of the most popular players in the NBA. Robinson's background in the Navy, his hard-working approach to basketball, and his highlight-film talent have made him a favorite not just with fans—but with teammates and opponents.

"David is the naval officer, helping to defend our country," said Orlando Magic general manager Pat Williams. "David is an educator and a motivator. He stands for goodliness. How can you attack that? Mister Robinson is who every family wants their son to become."[5]

Certainly, he is a son that has made his parents proud. Ambrose and Freda Robinson taught David from the beginning that there are more important things in life than being a star athlete. David learned those lessons well.

Chapter 2

A Different Kind of Kid

As a child growing up, David Robinson, his sister Kim, and his brother Chuck had the best kind of role models—their parents. Freda Robinson, his mother, was a nurse. Ambrose Robinson, David's father, was a Navy officer working as a sonar technician at a base near Norfolk, Virginia. Sonar is an electronic device that finds things under water by bouncing sounds off them.

From the start, the Robinsons realized that David was a very smart child. They told him that anything was possible if he worked hard enough. And they enrolled him in school programs for gifted children when he was seven years old. His favorite subject was math.

Ambrose Robinson said that when David was about eleven, his mother would take him to the store and use him to figure out how much different foods cost by the ounce. The young boy could add up the price of groceries faster than a calculator. By the time his mother reached the checkout line, David usually had the total bill figured out, right to the penny.[1]

David's mind got even quicker when he was a teenager. When David was fifteen, his father bought a kit for a six-foot projection TV. Before he could work on the kit, Mr. Robinson was sent to sea for three weeks. But while he was gone, David put the set together, all by himself. It worked perfectly. After that, David went down to the store that had sold his father the $1,800 television kit and helped fix a broken one there.[2]

Ambrose Robinson also taught his son how to play the piano at an early age. These days, David carries an electric keyboard with him wherever he travels. He finds it a good way to relax from the pressures of basketball. He plays everything from Beethoven to jazz to hard rock.

And David's parents taught him the value of hard work. He had a paper route and mowed lawns for several years.

Like most kids, David enjoyed sports. A left-hander, he played baseball, football, and tennis in local leagues. At age twelve, he won a golf tournament for his age group. Perhaps his best sport back then was gymnastics. He specialized on the parallel bars.

Basketball? That was not among David's favorites. He enjoyed watching the sport on television and rooted for the Philadelphia 76ers and their star, Julius Erving. But even though he was five feet nine inches in junior high, he quit the school team because he didn't especially enjoy it and thought that it interfered with his homework.

He didn't play again until his final year of high school. Shortly before that school year, Ambrose Robinson retired from the Navy and moved the family to Manassas, Virginia, a suburb of Washington, D.C. David, who had grown to six feet seven inches, was walking down the hall of his new school one day when he was spotted by guidance counselor Art Payne—who also happened to be the basketball coach.

David told the *Philadelphia Inquirer* that their conversation went something like this:

"Could you step in here for a moment, son?"

"Sure."

"Do you play basketball?"

"Around the playgrounds a little. I'm not in that good a shape."

"You want to play for me?"

"I'll give it a try."[3]

Even though he showed little interest in basketball, David was recruited for his high school team because of his height and athletic ability.

And so his career was born.

David was added to the team as the backup center and didn't expect to play much. But before the first game, the regular center was injured. David stepped in and scored 14 points with 14 rebounds. It was certainly an impressive debut.

David was almost always the tallest player on the court that year, and he had soft hands when catching or passing the ball. But he had no real knowledge of the game and poorly developed skills—mostly because he had not played much before. He liked the sport, but he didn't enjoy practicing. To him, basketball was just a game. It was not anything he expected to play after high school.

But others thought differently. College coaches from George Mason University, Harvard University, and Holy Cross University came to watch him play. All were interested in having him come to their schools. David was stunned. He didn't think he was that talented.

For the season, David's team won 12 games and lost 12. David averaged 15 points and 12 rebounds—good numbers, but not spectacular. That would have been the end of his career, except that one night one of the faces in the crowd belonged to Navy coach Paul Evans.

Evans had come to watch David play on the

advice of a naval officer who lived in the Robinsons' hometown. The coach was impressed. Here was a kid, Evans thought, with no real skills but with a lot of raw talent and desire. Soon after that, Evans was thrilled to learn that David had already applied to attend college at the U.S. Naval Academy in Annapolis, Maryland. The boy's plan was not to play basketball but to study electronics.

David thought that high school was too easy. He wanted to go to a college that would make him work harder. Plus he was eager to follow in his father's footsteps. If he could graduate from the academy, he figured, he would have a good start on the road to being successful.

David got in—because of his grades, not his basketball. The academy teaches men and women to run the Navy's ships and planes. They go to college for four years, graduate as naval officers, and then must serve in the U.S. Navy for up to five years. That sounded great to David.

But military life is not easy. When David got to Annapolis as a plebe (as newcomers are called), he quickly learned that he had to take orders from everyone: officers, teachers, older students. On a typical day, he would awaken at 7:00 A.M., do marching drills for an hour, and then go to classes for four hours. He would grab a quick lunch and then attend more classes through the afternoon. After dinner, he would have more marching drills and several hours of homework. Each night he went to bed exhausted.

Navy plebes are not allowed radios, televisions, or trips to the fast-food restaurants that David loved so much. In his dormitory, more than 130

FACT

Some of David Robinson's favorite things:

Food	Lasagna and chicken fajitas
Movie	"The Little Mermaid"
Hobby	Playing his keyboard and sax
TV Show	ESPN's "Sports Center"
Musician	Grover Washington, Jr. and Natalie Cole
Book	Bible
Athlete	Julius Erving
Hero	His father, Ambrose Robinson
Vacation	Relaxing at home

people shared one phone. But while some kids might resent that tough life, David grew to enjoy it.

His roommate, Carl (Hootie) Leibert, told *Sports Illustrated* magazine that "David loved the security of the place. He didn't mind someone telling him when to eat, sleep, work, play. The only negative was the lack of freedom. And David wasn't much of a partier, so he didn't need that."[4]

David also didn't really need basketball. He earned an A in gymnastics class and tried boxing for a while. His career in that sport ended quickly when he broke a bone in his pinkie during a bout. Finally, a few weeks before the basketball season began, he decided to go out for the team. Mostly, he thought, playing basketball would help take his mind off all the hard work and the marching.

Coach Evans had grander plans. He saw in David a youngster who had terrific raw talent but very little knowledge about basketball. It didn't hurt, also, that David was still growing. He had entered the Navy at six feet seven inches and seemed to be adding an inch every other month. Coach Evans thought that David had the chance to be a great player if he was willing to work hard enough.

Evans compared coaching David to coaching a ninth or tenth grader. "He's eager to learn," the

Though Navy coach Paul Evans spotted David's natural talent for basketball, few could have predicted he would later be a star in the National Basketball Association.

coach said. "He's only played the game for a few years, so he hasn't picked up many bad habits. He's a little timid, sometimes, but he'll get over that. He's capable of doing almost anything."[5]

In 1983–84, Robinson's first season at Navy, he spent most of each game on the bench. In practices, he usually played against Vernon Butler, the team's six-feet-seven-inch forward. Butler was called "Captain Crunch" because of his rough style of play. David didn't enjoy being pounded by Butler every day. But he quickly learned that, to survive, he would have to work hard too. It was a good lesson for the young player.

David played in twenty-eight games as a plebe, although he didn't start any. He averaged 7.6 points and 4 rebounds per game, nice numbers coming off the bench. Most impressive was his shooting. He made more than 62 percent of his field goal attempts, a terrific figure.

The Midshipmen, as Navy's team is called, had a great season. They won twenty-four games and lost just eight. It was the first time in history that the school had topped twenty wins in a season. Of course, with David Robinson there, they would reach that number four years in a row.

After that first season, Coach Evans sat Robinson down for a talk. He told the young player that

David realized that hard work and practice improved his playing skills, while at Navy. Today he continues to work hard in the NBA.

he had the chance to be one of basketball's best players. But David had to want it. And he had to be willing to work hard for it.

David thought about his coach's words over the summer. He came back for the 1984–85 season as a changed man. The growth wasn't just in his height—although he now stood about seven feet tall. The growth was also in his attitude. He decided to put his full efforts into basketball. He decided to see exactly how good a player he could be.

His improvement became obvious very quickly.

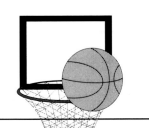

Chapter 3

Setting Sail

When the 1984–85 basketball season opened, few of the nation's coaches were talking about David Robinson. The preseason magazines barely mentioned him. He didn't make anyone's list of the top fifty players in college ball.

But the sophomore center from Navy launched a sneak attack on college basketball. He exploded on the scene like a torpedo. Within the first few games of the season, it became clear: Here was a powerful new force in the sport. Here was one of the country's best young players.

It wasn't just that David had grown four inches over the past year—although that certainly helped. The big difference was that he was learning to play the game. That might sound silly, but remember that David had barely played any basketball before his last year of high school. He had been years

David earned the nickname "The Aircraft Carrier," for being Navy's top shooter and rebounder. As center for the San Antonio Spurs, he again is team leader in scoring and rebounding.

behind his teammates in his knowledge of the sport. Now he was catching up—and fast. Following Coach Evans's advice, David dedicated himself to becoming a star. He devoted extra hours each day to learning the game. Each morning, he worked on his defense. Each evening, he worked on his shooting. Each night, he went to bed exhausted.

Beyond all the basketball, David had a grueling class schedule. As a "youngster," (which is what the Navy calls second-year students), he studied physics, computer science, calculus, and thermodynamics. (Thermodynamics is the study of how moving objects produce heat.) Most days, he also had marching drills. He was a soldier, a student, and a basketball player. It was a tall order to fill.

But David managed. And all the extra work he put in began to pay off. In the third game of the season, he scored 29 points and grabbed 11 rebounds in an 84–68 win over American University. Former Boston Celtics star Sam Jones was at the game and said of Robinson: "He's raw, but he's got a lot of talent. He's got a nice touch. He runs well. He's got some things to learn. But with his height and his finesse, he's a pro prospect."[1]

It was the first time that anyone had suggested that David could make it in the NBA. David himself laughed at the idea. But the more he played, the better he looked.

In the Saluki Shootout Tournament in December 1984, David was everyone's choice as most valuable player. In four games he scored 115 points and had 52 rebounds. And he earned a nickname: "The Aircraft Carrier." Why? Because he carried Navy to victory each game. The nickname would stick.

For the season, David averaged 23.6 points and 11.6 rebounds per game. He also blocked 128 of his opponents' shots, which led all players in the country. The Middies went 26–6. They were champions of the Colonial Conference. And, for the first time in twenty-five years, they went to the NCAA Championship Tournament.

That tournament features the sixty-four best college teams in the country. For David, it was another new challenge. Some experts were not so impressed by his great numbers because of the league in which he played. The Colonial Conference is known for having schools with tough academic standards, not with great basketball programs. Sure, Robinson had scored all those points, blocked all those shots, and grabbed all those rebounds. But skeptics said he had not done it against great players. Could he hold his own against the best? Absolutely.

In his first NCAA game, against Louisiana State

University, Robinson had 18 points, 18 rebounds, and 3 blocked shots. Navy won, to everyone's surprise.

Then the Middies played Maryland, which was among the top ten teams in the country. David showed his stuff less than ninety seconds into the game. When teammate Vernon Butler missed a layup, David clutched the ball as though it were a grapefruit and slammed it home. The next time down the floor, he turned on Maryland center Derrick Lewis and scored from eight feet. The time after that, he posted Lewis from six feet.

He was even more impressive on defense. In one brief stretch, Robinson blocked a shot by Lewis, another shot by Adrian Branch, and then tipped Len Bias's miss to a teammate.

For the night, he had 4 blocks and 8 rebounds. He was 11 for 18 from the field. In the end, however, Maryland won the game. Afterward, Robinson said he had played the game angry. Players from Maryland had not taken Navy seriously going into the game. David said, "I guess I have a little chip on my shoulder for Maryland. I wanted to show them I could play. I wanted their respect."[2] He earned it.

After that season, David faced a tough decision. He had to decide whether to stay at the Naval

Academy or switch to another school. If he transferred now, he could play two more seasons of college ball and then go directly to the pros. But if he stayed at Navy, he would have to serve five years in the military after finishing school. He would be at distant naval bases or on ships in the middle of the ocean. And that would almost certainly kill any chance he had of playing in the NBA.

Some of the country's top basketball schools let David know they would love to have him. That was appealing. So was the possibility of getting rich down the road. A top player in the NBA earns more than $1 million a year. As a naval officer, Robinson was promised nothing more than $24,000 a year, plus free food and housing. But money wasn't everything to David. He had gone to Navy because he wanted to become an officer, like his father. That career still appealed to him. Despite what many others said, he still wasn't convinced he could make it as an NBA star. And, most of all, he enjoyed his life at the academy. He figured, why change something that you like?

Overall, it was the trickiest decision David ever had to make. Just thinking about it kept him up at night. He sought the advice of his parents, his friends, and his teachers. He spoke with Navy officials, who hinted that—maybe later—they would agree to cut the number of years he had to serve. But they made no promises.

In the end, only he could make the choice.

In April 1985, Robinson announced his plans. He released a statement saying that his top priority was his education. His second priority was loyalty. For those reasons, he would stay at the academy, even if it meant he would never play in the NBA.

"If I get a chance to play pro basketball, that's

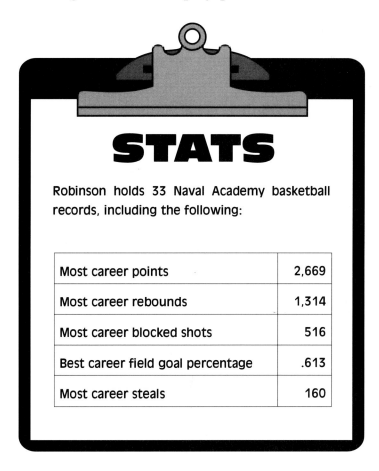

STATS

Robinson holds 33 Naval Academy basketball records, including the following:

Most career points	2,669
Most career rebounds	1,314
Most career blocked shots	516
Best career field goal percentage	.613
Most career steals	160

cool," he said. "But if I don't, it definitely won't break my heart."[3]

Many people praised Robinson as a national hero. He had chosen learning and loyalty over money. Others said he was foolish for letting the chance to become a millionaire slip through his fingers.

To many, David was a hero for choosing to finish his service in the Navy instead of turning professional.

David came back the next fall eager for his junior year (or, as the Navy calls it, his "Second-Class" year). He had spent the summer working on his toughness. He lifted weights and bulked up. Why? Because, tall as he was, David was skinnier than most of his opponents. Sometimes they could stop him by pushing him away from the basket.

He learned a few other things over that summer. For one, David taught himself to walk on his hands. He surprised his coach and teammates that fall by entering the gym for the first practice on his hands and walking that way across the entire basketball court. He also kept studying electronics and became an expert in fixing computers, TVs, or anything else that needed to be tuned up. Of course, coming back this season, Robinson wasn't going to catch anyone by surprise. Everyone in the country knew how great a player he had become. And everyone knew that Navy—once a basketball weakling—was now a strong team.

Both Navy and the San Antonio Spurs have Robinson to thank for turning their teams into winners.

But that didn't mean they could stop the "Aircraft Carrier." Navy won thirty of its thirty-five games, the best season in Naval Academy history. David was named an All-American after averaging 22.7 points and 13 rebounds a game. And all that time he spent working on his defense really paid off. He set NCAA records for most shots blocked in a game (14) and a season (207). In fact, only one team, national champion Louisville, blocked more shots (213) than David did by himself.

The Navy team's goal was to go further in the NCAA Tournament. But first, they had to face Syracuse University, the champion of the Big East Conference. Syracuse was ranked number seven in the country. Making matters tougher, Navy had to play the game in Syracuse. Even before the game, Navy's players had a good reason to be psyched up. A few of the Syracuse players had told a local newspaper that they would have no problem beating the Middies. Syracuse center Rony Seikaly called David and his teammates "shorthairs," an insulting reference to their close-cropped haircuts.[4]

Robinson was furious. He vowed to make Seikaly eat his words. Before the game, David told teammates that his goal was to hold Seikaly to 4 points.[5]

In fact, Seikaly finished with exactly 4 points,

shooting only 2 for 8. Both he and backup center Rodney Walker fouled out trying to stop Robinson. Meanwhile, in a magnificent performance, David scored 35 points, pulled down 11 rebounds, and blocked 7 shots. Once, Seikaly tried a shot, and David swatted it right back into his nose. The Middies pulled off a 97–85 upset over Syracuse before 21,713 stunned spectators.

Navy won another game, beating Cleveland State when David hit a game-winning shot with six seconds to go. The Middies finally lost to Duke University but were proud to finish in the final eight of the tournament.

A year earlier, Robinson had decided to stay at Navy partly because he wasn't sure he was good enough to become a pro. But after the success of his junior year, he began to see things a bit differently.

The better he got at basketball, the more it excited him. Maybe, he began to think, he could lead Navy to a national championship. There was one more season to go.

Chapter 4

Player of the Year

When David Robinson first made Navy's team as a freshman, he sat down and wrote his goals on a piece of paper. Before his college career was over, he wrote, he hoped to score 1,000 points. He hoped to grab 600 rebounds. And he wanted to play in the NCAA tournament.

David reached those goals early in his junior season. So he made out a new list.

Now, he wrote, he hoped to score 2,000 points, grab 1,000 rebounds, and be named an All-American player. It was, he thought at the time, probably more than he would achieve.

But David was an All-American as a junior and hit the other numbers early in his senior year. So he scribbled down his ambitions a third time. This time he wrote, "I want to be the best player in the country."[1]

Once again, he made it. By the time David's senior season was over in 1987, he was praised by everyone as the nation's top college player. He won all of the player-of-the-year awards. He even won the Sullivan Award, which goes to America's top amateur athlete, regardless of which sport he or she plays.

Everywhere David went, he was the center of attention. He played his best games against the top opponents in the big arenas with a lot on the line. In front of 23,000 fans at the University of Kentucky's Rupp Arena, Robinson single-handedly kept the Midshipmen in the game against the top-ranked team at the time. He had 45 points, 14 rebounds, and 10 blocked shots. Kentucky coach Eddie Sutton led the crowd in a standing ovation when Robinson was taken out with fourteen seconds left.

In another game against James Madison University, Robinson won the contest with two seconds left, throwing a forty-foot heave through the basket. He was carried from the court by classmates and fans.

David's final college game came in the NCAA Tournament against a tough University of Michigan team. Navy was way overmatched, but David did his best. He scored a career-high 50 points. He

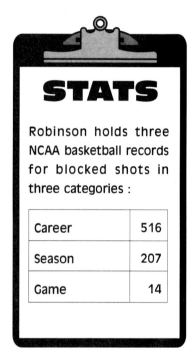

STATS

Robinson holds three NCAA basketball records for blocked shots in three categories :

Career	516
Season	207
Game	14

Robinson goes up to block a shot by the Golden State Warriors'
Mitch Richmond. By the end of his college career, he was being
compared to the best defensive players in the country.

left the game with two seconds to go and Navy way behind. He received a thunderous ovation from the crowd. Players on both teams lined up to shake his hand.

For the season, he averaged 28.2 points per game—third-best in the nation. His 11.8 rebounds per game was fourth, and his 4.5 blocks per game was first. In fact, his 516 career blocks was an all-time record for any college player.

Remember, as a freshman David had problems playing defense. Only through hard work was he able to improve. By the time he finished college, he was being compared with the greatest defensive player of all time—former Boston Celtics center Bill Russell. University of Indiana coach Bob Knight, who has been around the sport for forty years, said Robinson blocked shots and clogged the lane just like Russell once did. But, Knight added, Robinson was a better offensive player.[2]

Much as David had grown in height, he had also grown as a person. He began to realize that responsibility came with being a sports star. People looked up to him. He had to set an example.

When he accepted the 1987 Sullivan Award at a banquet in Washington, D.C., Robinson—wearing a crisp Navy dress uniform—took time out to sign autographs for dozens of children. In his speech, he

Robinson has tried to become a role model, teaching children to stay in school and away from drugs.

told the kids to stay close to books and far from drugs. He even began to sign his autograph with the note: "Stay in school, David Robinson."

As often as possible, however, Robinson tried to be by himself. The more that people knew him as a basketball star, the less sociable he became. He told reporters, "I used to love to talk to people. I loved to be around people all the time. But now I don't. I like my time alone. And I really appreciate my privacy much, much more. But things turned out for me real well the last two years. I can't complain at all."[3]

Of course, even when David's college basketball career ended, he wasn't through with the Navy. The rules said he had to devote five more years to military service.

But things were changing. A year earlier, Secretary of the Navy John F. Lehman, Jr., had allowed another academy sports star, football player Napoleon McCallum, to play for the Los Angeles Raiders while serving at a naval base in Long Beach, California. McCallum played in home games after his shift at the base was over. Maybe David could get a similar deal. He certainly hoped so.

Unfortunately, Lehman resigned from the Navy before he could decide on David. The new Navy secretary, James H. Webb, said there would be no more special treatment for athletes. McCallum had to quit the Raiders. Robinson could not play part-time for the pros—at least for now.

Webb did make one compromise. Because Robinson stood seven feet tall, he could not fit on the cramped navy submarines. Therefore, there was not a good reason to keep him around for the full five years. Webb decided that David would serve two more years. After that he could join the NBA.

David thought it was a fair decision. After all, he had joined the Navy expecting to serve all those years. And the Navy made it easier for him to swallow in two other ways. First, he could be drafted by an NBA team now, even if he couldn't play for two seasons. Second, he would be allowed to play in the 1988 Summer Olympics. In fact, David did not think he would be picked in the 1987 NBA draft. Why would a team take him now, he wondered, if it couldn't use him for another two seasons?

On NBA draft day—June 22, 1987—David went golfing with friends. He didn't expect anything to happen. But the San Antonio Spurs, who owned the first pick, viewed it differently. They wasted no time in announcing their choice—center David Maurice Robinson of the U.S. Naval Academy.

The Spurs needed David for several reasons.

First, they were one of the worst teams in the NBA. They also needed a center. And the Spurs had been losing fans. In 1982–83, they averaged just 8,000 fans per game, second-lowest among the twenty-three NBA teams. "Hopefully," Spurs owner Angelo Drossos said, "David will lead us to the Promised Land."[4]

David wasn't so sure. In his heart, he wanted to play for the Los Angeles Lakers or Boston Celtics, two of the NBA's glamour teams. The Spurs . . . well, he had never thought much about the Spurs. He had enjoyed building Navy's basketball program into a good one. Now he preferred to play for a team that already was a winner. And he had never been to San Antonio, a historic city about 150 miles from the Texas-Mexico border. Other cities interested him more.

Because he still had two years to serve in the Navy, Robinson was in no rush to sign with the Spurs. If he didn't sign with them during those two years, he could go back into the NBA draft in 1989. Then he would probably end up with a different team. The Spurs knew this. So they set out to impress David. They flew him to San Antonio, where 700 fans met him at the airport. They carried signs reading, "Say Yes, David." Mayor Henry Cisneros flew him on a helicopter tour of the city.

With two years away from basketball, Robinson had to work hard to get back in shape.

He was treated to a lobster dinner with several of the Spurs' young players.

David found himself liking San Antonio and the Spurs. But, of course, money was a big issue. No problem, said Drossos. The owner offered David an eight-year, $26 million deal. At the time, it was the biggest contract in the history of sports.

Robinson happily signed. But while the rest of the Spurs reported to training camp a few days later, David's dream of playing pro ball would have to wait. He was sent to a submarine base in King's Bay, Georgia, where he was just your basic seven-feet-one-inch navy man. His job was to supervise the building of submarines.

David soon found that he missed basketball. He played pick-up games at the base. But of course, there was no one close to his talent. That fall, he got to play for the U.S. team in the Pan-Am Games, a tournament among teams from different countries in North and South America. The time he had spent away from the game showed. He looked rusty. In the gold-medal game against Brazil, he fouled out with six minutes left, and the United States lost, 120–115.

He was looking forward more to 1988, when the Olympics would be held in Seoul, South Korea. David wanted to play for America's team there. In fact, he said, he wanted to lead the team to a gold medal.

In May of 1988, he showed up for Olympic tryouts. By his own admission, David was out of shape. After all, in the past year he had gone from averaging 28 points per game to averaging eight hours a day sitting behind a desk. He knew he had some catching up to do. So he got to work—running for four hours a day, lifting weights, swimming, scrimmaging. "I want to stand out," he said. "I just want to be able to run and keep up and run faster than anyone. I feel like I will be dominant when I go out and play."[5]

Olympic coach John Thompson expected the same. Robinson would be his "go-to" guy on the team, the coach said. He was expected to clog up the middle on defense and use his height to score points on offense. And with a supporting cast of college stars such as Danny Manning, Dan Majerle, and Hersey Hawkins, it seemed certain that the United States team would win it all.

Chapter 5

The Rookie Arrives

Only once in the history of the Summer Olympics had the U.S. men's basketball team lost a game. In fourteen previous Olympics, the United States had won the gold medal thirteen times.

So it seemed certain that the 1988 team—led by David Robinson and taught by Georgetown University coach John Thompson—would cruise to victory. No one was surprised when the team won its first six games. Robinson did his part. He was the team's top scorer and rebounder.

But there were problems along the way. Four of America's twelve players were injured and missed games. Other players, including Robinson, did not like Coach Thompson's strict ways. There were arguments between the coach and his players.

All of that wouldn't have mattered if the United States brought back the gold. But things fell apart in a game against the Soviet Union. The Americans took bad shots and threw sloppy passes. The Soviets, meanwhile, played a smart, careful game. When the buzzer went off in the end, David's team had lost, 82–76.

The American players were stunned. "We came to win the gold," Robinson said right after the loss. "I can't even describe my disappointment. We really wanted to win this game. We played hard all summer. We played hard in the Olympics. We just didn't play well tonight. We picked a bad night not to play well."[1]

The Americans recovered to beat Australia for the third-place bronze medal. But it was a major disappointment.

After that, many of David's Olympic teammates went straight to NBA teams. David, meanwhile, went back to the navy base in Georgia. He was itching to play basketball. But he knew he had just months to go now until he could join the Spurs.

In May of 1989, "The Admiral" was released from the Navy. He reported right to rookie camp in San Antonio. Things had changed since the club drafted him two years earlier. There were nine new players on the twelve-man roster. There was a new owner, Red McCombs, and a new coach, Larry

Robinson makes a layup. In his first game as a San Antonio Spur, Robinson scored 23 points against the Lakers.

Brown. And there was a new battle cry among fans: "Robinson has arrived!" After all, the club had won just 21 of 82 games the year earlier. Fans expected Robinson to double those wins just by himself.

David was eager to get started. He bought a condominium for himself and placed a grand piano in the middle of the living room. He also bought a house for his parents. Mr. and Mrs. Robinson would live nearby and handle David's business and personal matters. Their toughest job was meeting all the requests for autographs. About 1,500 letters would arrive each week asking for David's signature. David's mom joked that her house began to look like a post office.[2]

Mr. Robinson also began to keep a videotape library of all the Spurs games that were on TV. He would study the tapes and try to help his son sharpen his skills. After tough contests, father and son would sit down together, share some popcorn and soda, and relive the game on TV. Sometimes, Mr. Robinson said, his son would accuse him of being too bossy.[3]

David quickly made a best friend on the team. Forward Terry Cummings came to the Spurs that season in a trade with the Milwaukee Bucks. Like David, he liked to play the piano and sing. Like

David, he was crazy for Italian food. The two young men hung around together most of the time and even wrote songs during long plane flights. Cummings likes gospel music. David prefers classical. His favorite composer is Beethoven.

There were other new players. Caldwell Jones, a thirty-eight-year-old center, was brought in to back up Robinson at center and help teach David how to play NBA-style defense. Jones watched David in practice for a week and declared, "He has all the talent that all us big guys only hope and dream for."[4]

Maurice "Mo" Cheeks, a smart point guard, was hired to help run the offense. And Sean Elliott, a six-feet-eight-inch forward, was picked as the third pick of that year's draft.

Overall, there was great excitement when the Spurs opened the 1989–90 season. With "The Admiral" leading the charge, things seemed certain to improve.

David's first pro game came on Nov. 4, 1989, against the NBA champion Los Angeles Lakers. David later admitted that he had an upset stomach and threw up just before the game. But he blamed the problem on eating Mexican food and not on being nervous. Certainly, he didn't play as if he were nervous. David scored 23 points and grabbed

17 rebounds. The Spurs—NBA doormats the season before—beat the league champs, 106–98.

Word soon got out about the twenty-four-year-old rookie. After just a few months in the league, he was already being compared with Hakeem Olajuwon of the Houston Rockets and Patrick Ewing of the New York Knicks. Those two men were considered the best centers in the league.

What quickly set David apart was his speed and grace. Unlike most seven-footers, he can run as fast as the smaller players. That allows him to score points on the high-speed fast break. And he can make moves that few athletes—other than gymnasts—are able to make. That makes him a league leader in blocking opponents' shots.

What Robinson doesn't have is bulk. He weighs 235 pounds which, believe it or not, is small for a man standing seven-feet-one. It was feared when he joined the NBA that some of the massive giants playing center would simply shove David away from the basket. But as a rookie, he quickly showed he was able to bang bodies with men fifty pounds heavier—and live to talk about it.

Off the court, Robinson is a perfect gentleman. But to make it in the NBA, a player has to be tough. One time reporters asked Robinson to describe himself in a rough situation. He shocked everyone by

Robinson's light weight has not stopped him from going up against the heavyweights in the NBA.

saying, "I'm an animal when I smell blood. If somebody hits me I say, 'Hey, OK, you hit me, I hit you back.'"[5]

In one game against the Lakers early that season, Robinson was double-teamed by muscular center Vlade Divac and forward James Worthy. He was knocked to the floor several times early in the first quarter. But he got back up, streaked his way through the middle, and slammed the ball through the net over Divac's head. When the game ended, Robinson had more points than Divac and Worthy put together.

Describing the game afterwards, David said, "I got hit in the nose, the face. I almost got my eye knocked out by the Lakers. Most centers in this league play aggressively and outweigh me by many pounds. That means I have to get them moving. I have to make them match quickness for quickness."[6]

Most surprising was how quickly this rookie adjusted to the pros. After a two-year layoff, most people expected him to need a season or two to return to the level he had played in college. In fact, David worried about that himself. He had been in fewer than twenty real games in the past two years. How would he stand up in the NBA's rugged eighty-two-game schedule? And how would he do against much tougher opponents than he was used to?

But Robinson's rookie statistics were nearly identical to the ones he finished with at Navy. He averaged 24.3 points and 12.0 rebounds per game. His 3.9 blocked shots per game was third-best in the league.

San Antonio fans began to catch on. The club's attendance jumped by 30 percent that season, up to 14,700 per game. People were excited. It wasn't just that the Spurs were winning or that Robinson was such a great player. They were also turned on by his personality. Unlike some superstars, he was always approachable, always friendly. He was especially outgoing with kids. And once he got started, he was a world-class talker.

One time David agreed to a phone interview with a couple of high school journalists. He enjoyed the talk so much that he invited the two students to meet him in person after a game. Forty-five minutes after meeting with them, Robinson and the students were still chatting in the stands.[7]

David was chosen to play in the NBA All-Star Game as a rookie, a very rare honor. Playing alongside the likes of Michael Jordan and Magic Johnson, he scored 15 points and got 10 rebounds.

More important was how much he helped the

FACT

As a rookie, Robinson finished sixth in the NBA voting for Most Valuable Player. Here are the results:

PLAYER	PTS
1. Magic Johnson	636
2. Charles Barkley	614
3. Michael Jordan	571
4. Karl Malone	214
5. Patrick Ewing	152
6. David Robinson	102

Spurs. David led the team to its first division title in seven years. The club won fifty-six games—thirty-five more than it had the season before. That thirty-five-game improvement was the best in NBA history, three better than what the Boston Celtics did in 1979 with rookie Larry Bird.

The Spurs went to the playoffs that year, where they beat the Denver Nuggets, three games to zero. They went on to play the Portland Trail Blazers, who had finished the season with the NBA's second-best record. It was a tough series. Each team won its first three games at home. The seventh and final game was tied after forty-eight minutes and went into overtime. Robinson and Portland center Kevin Duckworth traded basket for basket. But with just seconds left, a Spurs' player made a bad pass and then a foul. The Trail Blazers won the game. The Spurs' season was over.

All in all, it had been a great year for David and his teammates. Robinson was voted the NBA's Rookie of the Year. He finished ninth in the league in scoring and second, behind Olajuwon, in rebounds. He had arrived—big time.

One coach who felt that way was Don Nelson of the Golden State Warriors. When it was over, Nelson told reporters, "I think we're looking at a David Robinson Era and it's starting right now. When he's

As a rookie, Robinson won many awards, including:

- NBA All-Star team

- Rookie of the year

- All-rookie team

- NBA All-Defensive second team

- All-NBA third team

- Schick Pivotal Player Award

Robinson led his team to the division title his rookie season. The Spurs were knocked out of the playoffs in the final game of the series against the Portland Trail Blazers.

finally finished, David Robinson will be right there with Magic Johnson, Larry Bird and Michael Jordan in terms of how much impact he has on the game."[8]

David would show more impact in his second season.

Chapter 6

Making a Name for Himself

Entering the 1990–91 season, there was great excitement around the Spurs. After Robinson's sterling rookie year, everyone wanted to know, what would he do now? How much better could he get? Plus, the Spurs kept making moves to improve the club. After their great improvement the year before, Coach Larry Brown didn't want to sit still. He wanted a team of players who could help David. He wanted players who would be able to work with the big, strong, fast center.

Brown found his guys. The 1990–91 club featured holdovers Terry Cummings and Sean Elliott—along with David. Another key player was shooting guard Willie Anderson. He had a knack of driving to the basket and snaking between taller defenders for layups.

San Antonio also needed a new man to run the

offense. Mo Cheeks, last season's point guard, missed his home in Philadelphia. He asked to be traded back East. So the Spurs sent him to the New York Knicks in return for Rod Strickland. Some experts thought that Strickland played a little out of control and was more concerned with his own points than with helping the team. But when he got to San Antonio, Strickland knew his job: Get the ball to the big man!

Overall, this was a strong and fast team with talented defensive players. So, while the Spurs

FACT

What a turnaround! The San Antonio Spurs made the biggest one-season improvement in NBA history in 1989-90, beating the 32-game turnaround the Boston Celtics made from 1978-79 to 1979-80. Here are some areas of greatest improvement:

Category	1988–89	1989–90
Record	21–61	56–26
Points allowed	112.8	102.8
Rebound percentage	.490	.519
Turnovers	21.1	17.1
Average home attendance	11,208	14,723

had shocked everyone a year earlier by winning the Midwest Division, this time around, no one was surprised. The team won fifty-five games, lost twenty-seven, and sold out every one of its home games.

After his outstanding rookie season, Robinson became the Spurs' team leader.

In the middle, of course, was The Admiral. In his second season, he led the entire NBA in rebounds and blocked shots. He scored more points than the year before. He made a higher percentage of his shots.

In fact, David seemed to be getting better game by game. One night, the Spurs were losing to the Los Angeles Clippers by just one point with fifteen seconds left in the game. Robinson snatched a pass on the right side. He didn't hesitate. He dribbled the ball down the court and drove for the hoop before being fouled. He made both free throws. San Antonio won the game.

Coach Brown was delighted. He told reporters that the season before, David would have settled for trying a jump shot. That would have been an easier play—but a tougher shot to make. "Now, he takes it to the goal," Brown said.[1]

David knew that the more respect he earned around the NBA, the more responsibility he would have to take with the Spurs. He was no longer a rookie who could get away with foolish mistakes.

Now he was regarded as a team leader. Now, he said, he had to play hard and play steady every night.[2]

The better David played, the more he drew comparisons with great players from history. Some said he resembled Kareem Abdul-Jabbar, the NBA's all-time leading scorer. Like Abdul-Jabbar, David is thin and fast. Both men could make athletic plays that leave other NBA centers in their wake.

But mostly experts compared him with Bill Russell, the Boston Celtics' center from 1956 to 1969. Those comparisons, you may recall, started when David was in college. But the better he got in the pros, the more people noticed the similarities. Both men are regarded as smart players who use their wits to get past opponents. Both are fast runners. Both jump quickly and have great timing while going up for rebounds.

Of course, there are a few differences. Russell was the greatest rebounder in history. Certainly, David has not reached that point. And Russell's team won an amazing eleven NBA championships during his thirteen seasons in the league. David's team has yet to win its first.

In Robinson's favor, he is probably a better offensive player. Russell never averaged more than 19 points per game in a single season. David, on the other hand, has never averaged fewer than 23.

One time, David was asked how he felt about being compared to Russell. He said, "I can't listen to that stuff. Bill Russell was a great player who played for a long time. I've just started. I feel like I have my own style. I'm still trying to figure out what it is, but it's unique from other players. Hopefully, I will create my own little niche in this league."[3]

A "niche" is a small area where someone fits in

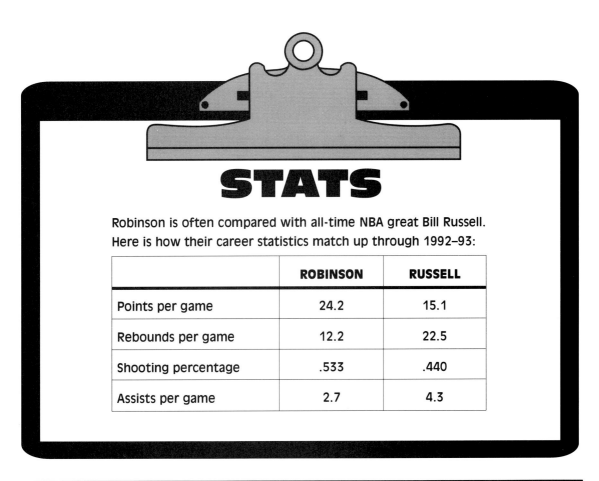

STATS

Robinson is often compared with all-time NBA great Bill Russell. Here is how their career statistics match up through 1992–93:

	ROBINSON	RUSSELL
Points per game	24.2	15.1
Rebounds per game	12.2	22.5
Shooting percentage	.533	.440
Assists per game	2.7	4.3

well. Where David fits in—just as where Russell fit in—is playing some of the best defense ever played by an NBA center.

Some players, be they kids or pro stars, are only happy when they're shooting the ball. Scoring is fun. It makes headlines and gets players on television. It's what most fans notice first. But defense wins games. If you can stop the other team from scoring, there is no way it can beat you. It is not surprising that the NBA's most-recent champions—the Detroit Pistons and Chicago Bulls—became known for playing tough, in-your-face defense. Even a great scorer like Michael Jordan knows that in order to make things happen, he has to play great when the other team has the ball.

Robinson feels the same way. One of his biggest thrills was being named to the NBA's all-defensive team in each of his first four seasons. In 1992, he was voted as the number one all-around defensive player among the 300 men in the NBA. It is no surprise, considering that he regularly blocks more of his opponents' shots than anyone around.

David said one thing that has helped him stuff opponents is the fact that he's left-handed. Because most people are right-handed, most players learn to make moves to the basket designed to beat right-handed defenders. When a lefty like

Being left-handed helps Robinson "stuff" his opponents.

David swoops in, the other guys are often unable to adjust.

One night in 1991, David beat the Orlando Magic by blocking eight of their shots. Afterward, frustrated Magic coach Matt Goukas said, "He does such a good job clogging the middle. He distorts your whole game."[4]

Another great example of his defensive skills came in a game against the New York Knicks and their roughneck center, Patrick Ewing. For the game, Ewing scored more points and had more rebounds than David. But down the stretch, David made two great plays. First, he stepped in front of a pass intended for Ewing, stole the ball, and started his team down the court for two points. Then, with nineteen seconds to go, he blocked Ewing's final shot. That sealed a four-point win for the Spurs.

Afterward, Ewing and Robinson met at half court to shake hands. It was a gesture of respect by both men.[5]

Respect is an important word in David Robinson's life. Respect for other players. Respect for himself. Respect for his coaches. Respect for his family. Respect for his country. Respect for his heroes.

One of Robinson's biggest heroes is jazz musician Grover Washington, Jr. David has spent hours

Knicks' center Patrick Ewing is one of Robinson's chief rivals.

and hours on his electric keyboard trying to play Washington's songs. He even bought a saxophone like Washington's and practiced on that difficult instrument.

So it amazed David to come home one day, flick on his answering machine, and hear Washington's voice. The jazz great had heard that David was a fan of his. He was a fan of David's. So before a concert in San Antonio, Washington called up, hoping the two men could get together.

David called Washington back, and they talked for an hour. Afterward David said, "I was just shocked that he knew who I was. He said, 'I love your work,' and all this stuff. It just never ceases to amaze me. I don't really think that what I do is all that great. I have fun doing it and everything, but it's so wild when other people know who I am."[6]

These days, there's no hiding the fact that David is a celebrity. When he goes to a shopping mall, he is surrounded by adoring fans. When he enters an arena, the applause rains down. He can't even go out for a pizza without attracting a crowd.

David doesn't mind the attention. He knows that it goes with the job and the high salary he makes. But, like everyone, sometimes he needs to get out of the spotlight. Over the years, he has found two ways to relax.

The first is sports—other than basketball. David is an excellent golfer, who averages in the 90s. And he may be the world's best seven-foot bowler. His average score is about 190, and he frequently tops 200. He also enjoys logic puzzles and computer games. Second, David is serious about his religion. He is a born-again Christian. Sometimes, after practices, he and a few teammates will discuss what they like about different religions. David has studied them all. Some teammates even jokingly called him "The Avenging Angel."[7]

As good as the 1990–91 season was for the Spurs, it ended on a sad note. After finishing first in their division, the club was expected to go far in the NBA playoffs. But in the first round, they ran into the Golden State Warriors. Led by star forward Chris Mullin, the Warriors shocked the Spurs, winning three games to one. Robinson averaged 25 points per game. He led both teams in rebounds. But once again, he went home disappointed.

He didn't stay home for long. David's rising stardom made him more and more popular. And it wasn't just among fans. He was also becoming a favorite among companies looking to sell their products. Soon, "The Admiral" would pick up a new nickname. Television viewers across the country would be invited into "Mr. Robinson's Neighborhood."

Chapter 7

NBA All-Star

The Nike sneaker company uses dozens of famous athletes in its commercials. One is David Robinson. He signed a $1-million deal to be a Nike spokesman when he joined the Spurs in 1989.

The company didn't need Robinson for its ads at that time. But in 1991—after David emerged as a top NBA star—Nike decided to run a series of TV commercials with him as the star. Nike took the popular kid's show, "Mr. Rogers' Neighborhood," and turned it into "Mr. Robinson's Neighborhood." David came on the ad as the host. He was trying to sell shoes, no doubt. But he also used it as an opportunity to talk to kids about other issues.

In one of the ads, David tried to sound just like Mr. Rogers. He looked into the camera and said, "Can you say garbage?" Garbage, he explained, was the word for the day. And in Mr. Robinson's Neighborhood, garbage is people who use drugs.[1]

That same year, David convinced Nike to start a "Stay-in-School" program aimed at high school students. The company printed millions of book covers urging kids not to drop out. The book covers were sent—free of charge—to schools across the country.[2]

Other companies came asking for David to sell their products. David agreed to a few. In each case, he insisted the sponsor agree to do something to help children in some way.

That's the kind of person he is. He cares about people, especially his family. Although David spends most of his days around grown men, his favorite times are when he is with his wife, Valerie, and their daughter. His favorite movie is a children's film, "The Little Mermaid," which he has watched dozens of times.[3]

David's kindness convinced many people that he would eventually replace Magic Johnson as the NBA's unofficial goodwill ambassador. He has the same kind of charm and good looks as Magic. And he may also be the smartest player in the league.

But make no mistake. Robinson is no softie. This David is a Goliath.

After the disappointing finish to the 1990–91

season, David vowed that the Spurs would improve. They might not win the NBA title the following year. But he wanted them to take the next step. He wanted them to go far in the playoffs.

The Spurs made just a few moves before that season. They picked up forward Antoine Carr in a trade with the Sacramento Kings. Carr's job would be to provide some muscle under the basket and help Robinson with the rebounds. And they signed sure-handed guard Trent Tucker for his outside shooting skills.

Off the court, David Robinson is a very caring person. He has helped start programs that encourage teenagers not to drop out of school.

From the start of the season, however, the Spurs went sour. Guard Rod Strickland, who had the job of running the offense, didn't think the club was paying him enough money. He refused to play in the first twenty-four games. San Antonio lost eleven of them.

Several other players went down with injuries early in the year. Halfway through the season, with San Antonio's record a disappointing twenty-one wins and seventeen losses, Coach Larry Brown was fired. A new coach, Bob Bass, was hired. His tough task was to turn around the season and get the Spurs into the playoffs.

At first, it appeared to be working. Bass gave his players more freedom to play the game as they wanted. Under his new system, the team turned its luck around. It won twenty-one of the first twenty-nine games Bass coached.

Through it all, David played like a star. In fact, he played like an all-star. The coaches and other players knew it. So did the fans. In 1992, they voted David in as the Western Conference starting center in the NBA All-Star Game. No other player received more votes from the fans.

This was Robinson's third all-star game in three years, and he loved it. First, it gave him a chance to play with and against the best basketball players in

Fans have overwhelmingly voted Robinson to the All-Star team every year of his NBA career.

the world. Second, the 1992 NBA All-Star Game was special. Magic Johnson, who had retired earlier that season after testing positive for the AIDS virus, was going to return for this one contest. David could hardly wait to team up with Magic.

David told reporters that he loved working with Magic, who was one of the best point guards in history. "He runs the floor great, he can see the cuts and he seems to like to pass it to me," David said.[4] He felt even better after the game, which the West won 153–133. Robinson hit 7 of 9 shots and scored 19 points.

Magic Johnson stole the show, scoring 25 points

FACT

In 1991, *Sports Illustrated* magazine asked 25 National Basketball Association coaches and general managers to name the league's best center. Here are the results:

1. David Robinson, San Antonio	20 votes
2. Patrick Ewing, New York	4 votes
3. Hakeem Olajuwon, Houston	1 vote

and taking home the most valuable player trophy. But David had his moments. Midway through the game, he found himself alone on the wing with Isiah Thomas. The Detroit Pistons guard is a full foot shorter than David. Both players smiled at the mismatch. Every time the speedy Thomas dribbled, Robinson reached out as if to swipe the ball. With a quick step, Thomas blew past Robinson. But David reached in with an extra long arm and stole the ball.[5]

Not many centers could have made that move. But not many centers are able to do as many things as Robinson does. When the statistics for the 1991–92 season were added up, David finished in the top ten in five different areas. He was first in blocked shots, fourth in rebounding, fifth in steals, sixth in shooting percentage, and eighth in scoring. In the history of the NBA, just two other players had finished that high in five categories. They were Cliff Hagen (in 1959–60) and Larry Bird (in 1985–86).[6]

With Coach Bass in charge and Robinson in top form, the Spurs were streaking toward the 1992 playoffs. But then disaster struck. In a game against the Charlotte Hornets, David jumped up for a rebound just as a Charlotte player was coming down. The two men crashed hands. David suffered a torn tendon in his left thumb.

At first, he tried to play with the injury. Two

Robinson looks to throw to an open man in the All-Star game.

nights later, against the Sacramento Kings, he covered the thumb with a plastic splint. It didn't hurt his rebounding. But he made just six of fifteen shots. The Spurs won anyway.

Three nights after that, David played against the Seattle SuperSonics. He led the team with 22 points and 14 rebounds. Better than that, he broke George Gervin's team record for most blocked shots in a career. It was the first of many Spurs records that Mr. Robinson would hold.

But the good times did not last. The pain in David's thumb grew worse each game. After playing in 232 straight games, he missed the first one of his career a few nights later. David took two weeks off, hoping he would heal. He didn't. Finally, he decided to have surgery. He realized that the chances of his thumb healing on its own were slim. But he also figured that if he had surgery, he would not be back for the playoffs.[7]

He was correct. David had his thumb fixed and missed the rest of the season. The Spurs, meanwhile, stumbled without their top star. They faced the tough Phoenix Suns in the first round of the playoffs and were knocked out, three games to none.

David used his time off to mend his thumb. He also took time to visit the Naval Academy. He had some old friends there, but mostly he wanted to see his younger brother. Chuck Robinson chose to follow David into the Navy and even play on the basketball team. At six-feet-five-inches, Chuck is not nearly as tall as David. But when the two men play one-on-one, guess who wins?

"I beat him," Chuck said. "I usually get him after we've just lifted weights, and he doesn't start taking it seriously until I'm up something like 6–2

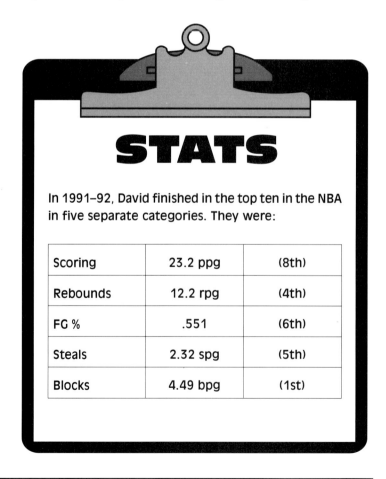

STATS

In 1991–92, David finished in the top ten in the NBA in five separate categories. They were:

Scoring	23.2 ppg	(8th)
Rebounds	12.2 rpg	(4th)
FG %	.551	(6th)
Steals	2.32 spg	(5th)
Blocks	4.49 bpg	(1st)

when we're playing to 8. But I've won more than I've lost."[8]

David had extra incentive to recover quickly. In just a few months, the Summer Olympics would begin. David had already been chosen for the Dream Team. It included eleven pro stars and one college player, Christian Laettner of Duke University. After the crushing loss in the 1988 Olympics, David was itching to get back. His teammates had not been to the 1988 Games, but they felt the same way. Said Larry Bird: "Our goal is to get to Barcelona, win the gold medal and bring it back where it's supposed to be."[9]

Few people had doubts about the Dream Team. But one man who wasn't so certain was Chuck Daly, the team's coach. Daly worried that a dozen superstar players might have a tough time working together. Each man, Daly said, was the top star on the team he came from. Each was used to taking the shot at crucial times of the game. How would they adjust to passing the ball at crunch time? How would these great players react to spending time on the bench?

Coach Daly had no need to worry. The Dream Teamers were more than happy to share the ball. They were content to sit on the bench and let their teammates get playing time. They all had the same goal—winning—and would not let their own egos get in the way of that.

In July 1992, America's Olympic team arrived in Barcelona, Spain. There were famous athletes all around, but the Dream Team drew the most attention. Everywhere they went, they were mobbed and asked for their autographs. Coach Daly compared it to traveling with twelve rock stars.[10]

There was just one problem. When the team arrived at its hotel in Barcelona, there were no beds large enough for Robinson and Ewing, the two seven-footers. Both men had to sleep with their feet hanging off the bed.

It may have been uncomfortable. But it sure didn't seem to hurt the way they played.

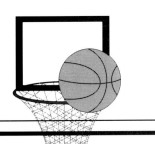

Chapter 8

A Gold Medal

From the first game of the 1992 Olympics, it was clear that no one could compete with the Dream Team. America's best players beat Angola, 116–48. The 68-point victory was the biggest rout in Olympic history.

Things didn't change much from that. The Dream Team topped Germany by 43 points. They whipped Brazil by 44. They creamed Lithuania by 51 points on August 6. That happened to be David Robinson's twenty-seventh birthday. He celebrated by scoring 13 points.

The huge wins actually had some fans complaining. Some said the NBA players were too talented to be playing against the rest of the world. They said the Dream Team should take it easy on its opponents. Robinson disagreed. He told reporters, "If you've got the best players in the world,

Robinson goes for the dunk against the Detroit Pistons.

send the best players in the world. This is sports, man."[1] In other words, the Americans would be cheating everyone if they eased off.

If the Dream Teamers weren't challenged by the rest of the world, they certainly challenged each other. The roughest contests didn't come in the games against other countries. They came in America's practices. The Dream Team would split in half—six men per side. And the world's best players would go at it for hours on end. Charles Barkley would try to dunk it over Karl Malone. Magic Johnson would try to steal the ball from Larry Bird.

FACT

In 1991–92, David was chosen as the NBA's top defensive player. The members of that season's all-defensive team were:

David Robinson, Spurs	Center
Michael Jordan, Bulls	Guard
Joe Dumars, Pistons	Guard
Dennis Rodman, Pistons	Forward
Scottie Pippen, Bulls	Forward

David Robinson and Patrick Ewing would bang bodies together under the backboard, each trying for the rebounds. The desire to win in these practices was unbelievable, David said. The skill level was mind-boggling. It almost was like watching an NBA title game.[2]

Put together, those twelve players cruised to a gold medal. They won all seven of their games. No opponent came closer than thirty-two points. After the Dream Team beat Croatia in the final game, everyone agreed that this was the greatest team assembled in history. Never again would people see the likes of it.

The Olympics were thrilling for David. This was his first championship since high school. But as soon as they ended, he knew he had to prepare for the 1992–93 season. Playing for San Antonio was his job. This was no time for a letdown.

David didn't know it then, but his fourth NBA season would be his wildest. Coach Bob Bass decided beforehand that he didn't want the job. So the Spurs hired their third coach in less than a year. He was Jerry Tarkanian, whose nickname was "Tark the Shark." Tarkanian was a successful college coach from the University of Nevada at Las Vegas. Over the years, he had won 625 games and lost just 122. At age sixty-two, this would be his first pro team.

Coach Tarkanian got the team off to a fast start, winning five of the first seven games. But there were problems. David was exhausted from playing in the Olympics. As hard as he tried to do well, he did not play up to his usual standards. And Tarkanian, who was used to winning nearly every game, could not adjust to the NBA. In the pros, even the best teams lose a good share of their games. That was a tough thing for the new coach to accept.

The Spurs dropped nine of their next thirteen games. That was more losses than Coach Tarkanian had in three whole years at Las Vegas. "The Shark" was so upset that he ended up ill. He had to be hospitalized for a few days. When he came back, he started arguing with San Antonio owner Red McCombs. Tarkanian said that he needed more players, especially a new point guard. McCombs disagreed. The owner believed that the Spurs had enough talent to win in the NBA.[3]

The two men continued to argue. So on December 18, 1992, Coach Tarkanian was fired. He had lasted just twenty games, less than a quarter of the season. David was disappointed. He liked Tarkanian as a coach and as a man. More than anything, he wanted stability. That means he wanted things to stop changing every few months.

He wanted the club to have one coach who would stay there for years and grow with the players.[4]

Would the next coach be that man? It is still too early to tell. But judging by the results John Lucas got during his first year in San Antonio, he could be the coach that leads the Spurs to an NBA title.

Coach Lucas was hired one day after Tarkanian was fired. San Antonio players did not know what to expect. Would he be a tough coach? Would he be easygoing? What kind of basketball would he want the team to play? What would he demand from his players? Lucas gave them the answers in his first game. With the Spurs down a few points early on to the Denver Nuggets, the coach called a time out. He got his players together and told them to get the ball to Robinson more often. David was the team's best player, Coach Lucas said. He should be taking the bulk of the shots.

Then the coach turned his eyes to Robinson. He told David that if he wanted to be a superstar, he had to work like one. Sure, David was still tired from the Olympics. But he had to get over that. The time to start, Lucas said, was now—in this game.

"We've got the best center in basketball. I believe that," Lucas said. "But we've got to make it trouble coming into David Robinson's neighborhood."[5]

David's teammates saw this and were impressed. If the new coach would demand that the Spurs best player work harder, then they knew they must all work harder. Guard Avery Johnson said Lucas's words were like a wake-up call for the entire team.[6]

The wake-up call was answered. The Spurs came back to beat the Nuggets in that contest. In fact, they won twenty-three of their next twenty-seven games. The whole team—and David in particular—was playing its best basketball in years.

Lucas is certainly not the typical NBA coach. Like many, he was once a star player, who spent fourteen seasons in the league. But unlike most, Lucas was once a drug addict. As a young man, he got hooked on cocaine. It ruined his game. And it ruined his life.

Coach Lucas worked hard to overcome that addiction. Once he kicked the habit, he worked to help other drug abusers. He opened a treatment center. He taught people that in order to solve their problems, they have to become responsible for their own actions.[7]

That idea works in life. And it works in basketball. As part of his plan, Lucas chose three veteran players and named them co-coaches. David was in charge of the group. The other members were forward Sean Elliott and guard Dale Ellis. If the Spurs wanted to

Coach John Lucas has pushed Robinson and the Spurs to play the best basketball in the team's history.

win, Coach Lucas said, it was up to these three players. During time-outs, he let them call the plays. If another player broke team rules, he let them handle it. If a trade was to be made, he asked for their ideas.

Most coaches simply tell players what to do. David loved that the new coach was giving him and the others some responsibility. He said it made him feel like a part-owner of the team. And when players feel like this is their team, he said, it makes them even more eager to win.[8]

The results were sure impressive. After their slow start, the Spurs finished the 1992–93 season with a 49–33 record. They went into the playoffs hoping to avoid the early knockouts they had suffered the past two seasons.

In the first round, they faced the Portland Trail Blazers. The Blazers were a talented club. The season before they had gotten to the NBA finals. But this time, the Spurs were prepared. The two teams split the first four games. Whichever one won the fifth game would take the series. Some players would be nervous going into that contest, but David told reporters, "It feels great. I've always enjoyed big games like this."[9]

He sure did. Robinson scored 20 points, grabbed 17 rebounds, and dished out 11 assists. Still, the game was tied after regulation. With less than one minute left in overtime, David snaked past Portland forward Cliff Robinson to score on a layup. That gave San Antonio the lead for good.

The win was thrilling. It gave San Antonio the series. Next, the Spurs had to face the Phoenix Suns, who had finished the regular season with the NBA's best record. The Suns were led by Charles Barkley,

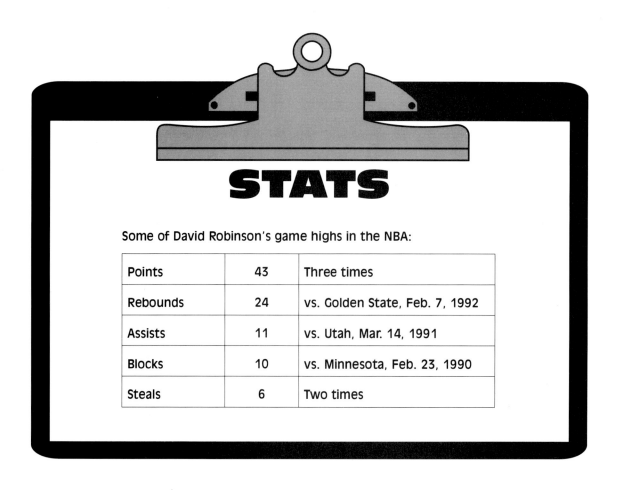

STATS

Some of David Robinson's game highs in the NBA:

Points	43	Three times
Rebounds	24	vs. Golden State, Feb. 7, 1992
Assists	11	vs. Utah, Mar. 14, 1991
Blocks	10	vs. Minnesota, Feb. 23, 1990
Steals	6	Two times

Up for the jump shot, Robinson goes over Phoenix Suns' forward Charles Barkley for three points.

the bulldozing forward who was the league's most valuable player that year.

This series, too, was very close. In game four, "The Admiral" dropped anchor on the Suns. David scored 36 points, while Barkley had just 18. He used his height and quickness to rule under the boards and win the game.

In the end, however, Barkley and his teammates had too much talent. The Suns won the series, four games to three. Phoenix would go on to win the 1992–93 NBA western conference championship.

Once again, David's season ended earlier than he had hoped. But he was excited going into 1993–94. The Spurs had a solid corps of young players. And, for the first time since Robinson arrived in San Antonio, the team had a smart coach who appeared ready to stay there for the long haul.

David now has several goals in life. He wants to be there for his wife and child. He wants to keep helping his country. That may come through working on antidrug programs. Or it may just come by being there to listen when kids want to talk.

His final goal is to win another championship. The Olympic gold medal in 1992 was sweet. An NBA title would be just as sweet. After four seasons of falling short, you would think he might be disappointed. But David sees it all as a growing

Star center David Robinson will continue to lead the Spurs in their pursuit of the NBA championship title.

experience, much like his years in the Navy. "For me, I've been learning a lot of things in these first few years," he said. "You know, it took Michael Jordan seven years to get a championship."[10]

Michael Jordan now has three championship rings. Before David Robinson is through, you can believe his fingers will have a few rings also.

Notes by Chapter

Chapter 1

1. Diane Pucin, "Cuba Does Get the Picture, U.S. Wins Opener by 79 Points," *Philadelphia Inquirer* (June 29, 1992), p. E1.

2. Stan Hochman, "Dream Scheme Isn't All Bad," *Philadelphia Daily News* (July 23, 1992), p. 6.

3. Mary Schmitt, "A Juggernaut Cast in Bronze," *St. Paul Pioneer Press* (July 24, 1992), p. 3G.

4. Glen Macnow, "20 Questions Inquisitive Fans Want to Know," *Street & Smith's Pro Basketball 1992–93* (New York: Cordé Nast Publications Inc., 1992), p. 100.

5. Bill Glauber, "Robinson Growing into Celebrity Status," *Baltimore Sun* (February 17, 1991), p. 1C.

Chapter 2

1. Jere Longman, "With a 6-11 Middie in the Ranks, Navy's Running Full-Speed Ahead," *Philadelphia Inquirer* (February 4, 1985), p. 11H.

2. Ibid.

3. Ibid.

4. Hank Hersch, "Anchors Aweigh," *Sports Illustrated* (November 19, 1986), p. 28.

5. Ken Denlinger, "At 6-11, Robinson Might Have Outgrown Navy," *Washington Post* (March 18, 1985), p. 81.

Chapter 3

1. Jere Longman, "With a 6-11 Middie in the Ranks, Navy's Running Full-Speed Ahead," *Philadelphia Inquirer* (February 4, 1985), p. 11H.

2. Ken Denlinger, "At 6-11, Robinson Might Have Outgrown Navy," *Washington Post* (March 18, 1985), p. B1.

3. Hank Hersch, "Anchors Aweigh," *Sports Illustrated* (November 19, 1986), p. 28.

4. Ray Parrillo, "Robinson and Navy Shock Syracuse," *Philadelphia Inquirer* (March 17, 1986), p. 1D.

5. Ibid.

Chapter 4

1. Dave Sell, "Paying Dues and Earning Commission, Ensign Robinson Eyes Future," *Washington Post* (May 17, 1987), p. D1.

2. Billy Reed, "On Court and Off, Robinson About the Best He Can Be," *Lexington Herald Leader* (January 23, 1987), p. D1.

3. Sell, p. D1.

4. Gordon Edes, "Spurs Going all out for Robinson," *Los Angeles Times* (September 27, 1987), p. D1.

5. Jere Longman, "Return to Form a Tall Order for Navy's Robinson," *Philadelphia Inquirer* (May 15, 1988), p. 3D.

Chapter 5

1. Mitch Albom, "16-Year Wait Turns Sour," *Detroit Free Press* (September 28, 1988), p. 1C.

2. Jere Longman, "Robinson has Spurs Shipshape," *Philadelphia Inquirer* (April 25, 1990), p. 1E.

3. Associated Press, "Robinson has a Real Family of Coaches," *Lexington Herald-Leader* (May 12, 1990), p. 4D.

4. Jack McCallum, "Hands On," *Sports Illustrated* (January 29, 1990), p. 21.

5. Rick Bonnell, "Robinson Spurred by the Hunt," *Charlotte Observer* (December 26, 1989), p. 1E.

6. Ibid.

7. Scott Howard-Cooper, "Spurs' Robinson Zooms to NBA Stardom," *St. Paul Pioneer Press* (February 4, 1990), p. 1D.

8. Jason Cole, "Robinson Era Dawning in NBA," *Peninsula [Calif.] Times Tribune* (March 2, 1990), p. 1E.

Chapter 6

1. Rich Hofmann, "Spurs' Ship is Coming In," *Philadelphia Daily News* (February 27, 1990), p. 75.

2. Ibid.

3. Corky Meinecke, "The Center of Attention, Robinson Spurs San Antonio," *Detroit Free Press* (March 15, 1990), p. 1D.

4. Bruce Newman, "Horn of Plenty," *Sports Illustrated* (April 22, 1991), p. 70.

5. Jack McCallum, "Hands On," *Sports Illustrated* (January 29, 1990), p. 19.

6. Bill Glauber, "Robinson Growing into Celebrity Status," *Baltimore Sun* (February 10, 1991), p. 1C.

7. Peter Finney, Jr., "Robinson an Avenging Angel," *New York Daily News* (November 19, 1991), p. 67.

Chapter 7

1. "Is David Robinson the Next Ad Superstar?," *San Jose Mercury News* (May 20, 1991), p. 11F.

2. Mike Antonucci, "Book Covers Free to Schools," *San Jose Mercury News* (August 19, 1991), p. 2C.

3. Tom Powers, "Admiral, Admirable—Robinson is Both," *St. Paul Pioneer Press* (January 17, 1992), p. 1D.

4. Tom Sorensen, "Another Magic Moment," *Charlotte Observer* (February 10, 1992), p. 1E.

5. Ibid.

6. San Antonio Spurs, *1992–93 Media Guide* (San Antonio: Spurs Publishing, Inc., 1992), p. 59.

7. Rick Bonnell, "Thumb Injury May End Robinson's Season," *Charlotte Observer* (March 26, 1992), p. 3E.

8. David Ginsburg, "Another Mr. Robinson in Navy Neighborhood," *Philadelphia Inquirer* (February 9, 1992), p. 8E.

9. Mary Schmitt, "A Juggernaut Cast in Bronze," *St. Paul Pioneer Press* (July 24, 1992), p. 3G.

10. Steve Love, "Olympic Spirit is But a Dream," *Akron Beacon Journal* (July 26, 1992), p. E1.

Chapter 8

1. Phil Jasner, "Battle Cry: Robinson Decries Lack of Support," *Philadelphia Daily News* (July 29, 1992), p. 76.

2. Diane Pucin, "It's Just Between U.S.: Basketball Practice a Dream Game," *Philadelphia Inquirer* (July 23, 1992), p. 1D.

3. Kelly Shannon, "Tarkanian Out of a Job Once Again," *Long Beach Press-Telegram* (December 19, 1992), p. C1.

4. Ibid.

5. Bob Ford, "With the Spurs, John Lucas Takes on Another Challenge," *Philadelphia Inquirer* (December 27, 1992), p. E6.

6. "Lucas is Already Showing an Unusual NBA Coaching Style," *Akron Beacon Journal* (December 24, 1992), p. C2.

7. S. L. Price, "A Success Story Returns," *Miami Herald* (February 26, 1993), p. D1.

8. Bob Ford, "For Spurs' New Coach, Character is What Counts," *Philadelphia Inquirer* (February 18, 1993), p. F1.

9. Associated Press, "Spurs Regain Winning Touch," *Wichita Eagle* (May 9, 1993), p. 11G.

10. David Moore, "Robinson Hears Boos at Home—Fans Frustrated by Spurs' Strange Season," *San Jose Mercury* (April 28, 1993), p. 6D.

Career Statistics

Year	Team	G	FG%	REB	AST	STL	BLK	PTS	AVG
1989-90	Spurs	82	.531	983	164	138	319	1,993	24.3
1990-91	Spurs	82	.552	1,063	208	127	320	2,101	25.6
1991-92	Spurs	68	.551	829	181	158	305	1,578	23.2
1992-93	Spurs	82	.501	956	301	127	264	1,916	23.4
1993-94	Spurs	80	.507	855	381	139	265	2,383	29.8
TOTAL		394	.527	4,686	1,235	689	1,473	9,971	25.3

Where to Write David Robinson:

Mr. David Robinson
c/o San Antonio Spurs
600 East Market Street,
Suite 102
San Antonio, TX 78205

Index